AF256082

Men's Point Of View

A Snapshot In Time

ARLOA JANE WALTER

Author of "Voices of Older Women"

CARNEROS PRESS
Sonoma, California

ISBN 978-0-9701030-3-1

Published by
Carneros Press
PO Box 2051, Sonoma, CA 95476
www.carnerospress.com

Greg Walter, Editor & Publisher

Printed in the United States of America

First Edition

9 8 7 6 5 4 3 2 1

DEDICATION

This book is dedicated to the men in my life…

My husband of many years who has supported me in all I do…

My three sons and their families, and what is ahead for them…

My five brothers and all they bring to life…

My father, who died at a young age; I never really got to know him.

To all the men I interviewed, in particular, the one who first inspired me to get curious about men and what they were thinking. They have the experience, advice, and words of wisdom waiting to be shared with their families and the world.

This is just the beginning of telling their "life story." Cheers to their future beyond a "Snapshot in Time." My hope is that they will continue to share their story and words of wisdom to the world, because the world needs to hear from them. I wonder what is ahead for some of the younger men.

The book is about what I learned, what I thought I knew, what I know now and what I'll never know about men.

ACKNOWLEDGEMENTS

First I would like to acknowledge the men I interviewed. I thank them for the privilege of hearing their stories. They took the time to answer questions that pried into their lives, thoughts, ideas, and opinions. They were open, gracious and helpful. Special thanks to a couple of them who took a personal interest and offered advice.

This book was a "must do" for me—a journey with many stops and starts and ups and downs, but thanks to the men I interviewed I was able to keep going. It was to be a counterpart for the book I had written on women, *Voices of Older Women What They Want To Say… Why You're Not Listening.*

I had continued encouragement from family and friends. Thanks to the ladies in the Morning Glories Group, Andy McMurtrie, Beth McMurtrie, Nancy Nash-Lund, Maggi Forte, Penne Cosgrove, and Kay Narron.

Thanks to the women and men who referred men to me for interviews.

Thanks to my husband, who kept encouraging me, offered help and assistance, and most significantly, patience with me.

Thanks to my editor-and-publisher-son Greg Walter, who once again supported and helped me through a new project.

Thanks to the community of Lincoln Hills. Living here in this unique community where the aging experience is something to enjoy, benefit and grow from, and take pride in, while pursuing hobbies, favorite things, and reflecting on one's life.

CONTENTS

FOREWORD

I have known the author all of my life—she is my mother.

I am the eldest of her sons and at 56 years old, I am approaching the age group she focuses on here, it seems, at the speed of light. I am also the editor of this book, our second such collaboration.

Men's Point of View is not only a collection of interesting stories, observations and anecdotes from 34 individual men, I also hope that it is a catalyst and a reminder to anyone who reads it.

It can be a catalyst in the sense that I believe that anyone who reads this book will likely find themselves beginning to think about their own lives and start to remember things undone and unsaid. In essence, I believe that this book can launch or continue a life review process for each reader. I found myself doing exactly that as I was editing the final versions of this book.

I not only think that this is a good thing, I would urge anyone who finds themselves motivated to review their lives to simply go with it and embrace it. We leave many things unsaid and undone in our lives and any steps we can take to reconcile those things with ourselves and others will ultimately make our lives—and the lives of those around us—better and more fulfilling.

I hope that this book also serves as a reminder to all of us that first, we all have people in our lives—parents, grandparents, older friends—who perhaps need someone to listen to their stories, to help them share their wisdom and life lessons. We should all be willing and supportive listeners. Second, I hope it is a reminder to us all that life is short and extremely unpredictable. Take the time now to say what is unsaid and do what is undone.

Greg Walter
March 2014

**Excerpts from the poem
"And Then It Is Winter,"
author unknown:**

You know… time has a way of moving quickly and catching you
unaware of the passing years. It seems just yesterday that I was
young, just married and embarking on my new life with my mate. Yet
in a way, it seems like eons ago, and I wonder where all the years
went. I know that I lived them all. I have glimpses of how it was back
then and of all my hopes and dreams.

How did I get here so fast?
Where did the years go and where did my youth go?

Yes, I have regrets. There are things I wish I hadn't done...things I
should have done, but indeed, there are many things I'm happy to
have done. It's all in a lifetime.

You have no promise that you will see all the seasons of your life...so,
live for today and say all the things that you want your loved ones to
remember...and hope that they appreciate and love you for all the
things that you have done for them in all the years past!!

PREFACE

"Why a book on these older men? Because they have value. They have wisdom. They have learned lessons, worked hard, and have experienced so much. They could teach and direct and advise the younger generation… They are husbands, fathers, grandfathers, brothers, sons, friends and neighbors. They have so much to say…"

Older men who have reached retirement age are special. They have "been there, done that" and now have the time, ways and means to do what it is they really want to do. They have wisdom, experience, and strength and lessons learned, gained from living their lives. They have ideas and truths to pass on to their families and to the community and world. They are an untouched resource for their families and the world.

The idea for this book really started a while ago. I was out for my morning walk and ran into a man named Elliot I have seen him on my morning walks for the past few years. We always said hello and wished each other a nice day. As time went on we had a few more things to say—small talk, normal life stuff—about his wife playing golf, that he had hurt his heel, that he had seen his grandchildren who live nearby, and soon we introduced ourselves.

So, that day Elliot and I were talking and I wondered out loud about the people we both used to see while walking. He said he still saw one or two at times and that the others had probably died. He went on to say that eight men on his street had died one after the other. I looked at him and asked, "Wow, how do you handle that?"

He said sadly, "That's just what happens. You get old and then you die."

There was something in his voice and in his eyes that made me want to know more about what he was thinking. I wanted to hear more about the way he was feeling. At that moment I thought about the book I had written a couple of years before. It was called *Voices of Older Women* and it was about the largely ignored population of older women in our society—women who had so much to say, and so much to contribute and yet no one who would listen. I interviewed 100 women for that book—and while I was talking to Elliot I decided I wanted to interview him.

I remembered when I had my first speaking engagement after *Voices of Older Women* was published. Afterwards, a man came up and asked me when I was going to do a book about men. I told him then that I didn't know. But after speaking with Elliot, my immediate thought was that writing a book about men was an inspiration and the perfect follow-up to the work I had done with women.

Men's Point of View is an attempt to discover what retirement-aged men think about their lives, their family, the younger generation, men and women, careers and work, society, current affairs, retirement, and the personal stories about how they got where they are and what they have to say to the world.

Voices of Older Women came about because of my years of professional work with the older population, especially older women. I talked to women mostly in my community (Lincoln Hills, a senior community outside of Sacramento, Calif.) but also many outside of the community—100 in all ranging in age from 50 to 95 years old. I found that some felt that they were neglected, disrespected, unacknowledged, and forgotten as they got older. The women had suffered many losses—youth and beauty in a youth and beauty dominated world, families that grew up and moved away, spouses through divorce and death, and jobs because they retired. I found that these women really wanted to talk. They had much to say about their journeys and how circumstances had brought them to retirement—30 years or so to live with no guidelines, direction or in many cases anyone to share it with. These women often took up new careers and found new friends and accepted their new lives.

After my conversation with Elliot, I decided I wanted to interview older men and see whether their experiences were the same or different. I didn't know what to expect with the men but immediately found the whole process much more difficult. First, it was harder to find men to interview. Second, these older men were not as talkative or expressive as the women. But I knew that they all had a story to tell, so I designed a questionnaire and went ahead. I interviewed 34 men, almost all residents of Lincoln Hills.

Lincoln Hills is a unique community in many ways; the men and women who live here have chosen to move to a senior community away from the average everyday neighborhoods, exclusively senior populated—no one under 55, relatively well to do—as most have sold a home and have some assets and are free to do what they want to do.

Interviews

The interviews started with a few men I had come to know living here in Lincoln Hills, then continued after talking about the project to some of the women I knew. They gave me some referrals, but the process was very slow. In the end I interviewed 34 men. We would meet at my home or at theirs if they preferred. I had prepared a questionnaire with about 60 questions. The interviews usually lasted between 45 minutes and one hour.

There were seven men in their 80s, 15 men in their 70s, 10 in their 60s and two in their 40s. Most lived in Lincoln Hills while a few lived in the surrounding area. Most were retired although a few still worked part time. Most had time to reflect on their lives as well as check out all the activities here. All the names of the men have been changed to preserve their privacy.

Life Review

I'm not sure exactly how or why it happened but as I was interviewing the men and listening to them, and then later as I wrote this book, the concept of Life Review invaded my thoughts. Briefly it is a process that older persons take on consciously or not, at a certain time in their lives and it consists of looking back at their lives and relationships, noticing what is finished and also what is not, and realizing that what is not finished can be amended or changed. Then they can move on to accepting their lives and taking pride in them. They can start telling their stories to family and the community. This is all a part of the developmental stages we all go through in our lives according to psychologist Erik Erikson and others. There is much more on this subject later in the book.

This concept was not apparent to me when I interviewed the women for my previous book, *Voices of Older Women,* possibly because we talked easily about everything. With the men, who seemed to be more guarded and not so talkative, there seemed to be some missing parts. As I read more about the life review concept, I thought it could and should be a part of the natural progression of retirement in life, when there is time to reflect on things as well as to participate in all the activities and hobbies and interests one wants to explore.

There were some questions in the questionnaire, especially in the "Off the Cuff" section that seemed to encourage and elicit some of the life review naturally. In thinking about this I can say that it could at least have represented the start of the life review process for the men I interviewed because the questions triggered some memories and issues for some.

This is how and why the concept of life review came to be such an important part of the book. We are all doing it at some level after retirement and as we get older.

Retirement… Or Finally Just Doing What They Want To Do?

Compared to their fathers and grandfathers, many men now retire early and will live as a retired person far longer, depending on their individual situation. In past generations, the average lifespan was shorter and some men died as early as 40. Work was also different—far more physical in nature. Men did not have the options they do now and maybe did not have the extra money for travel and pleasure.

Looking at retirement now is different than it was even a decade ago. In the past, men in their 70s and older worked hard and when it was time to retire, they did. Generally, there was no choice and besides, they were tired. It was time and it was the thing to do. Once retired, one could travel, move, take up a new hobby or go fishing. Some would not want to get involved with a new hobby but would enjoy just not getting up every day for work, could sit and enjoy the free time. Others would join a club, serve on a committee, or decide to see the world if they could afford it and many could. They have saved for retirement without thinking much about it and also on their jobs the company often paid into it.

Of course there are a couple of really big issues that can affect and change all of the above. If the person is struggling to make ends meet or with very little income, when that income dries up he can be really devastated and unhappy. The other key issue is health. If one or one's spouse is ill with a chronic condition or suddenly has a stroke or heart attack or any other debilitating condition he is also in a different category and will feel age very soon or at least much before a person who is healthy. Illness can make one feel old very quickly. I refer to this phenomenon as "The Other Side of The Rosy Story" and it is addressed later in the book in Chapter 9.

All of these men have ideas, suggestions and comments on the family, younger generation, and differences between men and women, society, the hot topics of the day. They all have things they would do if they had the influence and power to change things. They all have families with which they are involved or not. Many are married for the second and third time, and only two were widowed.

Their comments are worth writing about for the world to see. Their personal responses are also something for them and their families to see. Just the idea of answering the questions, and letting me hear about their lives is in itself enough to put down on paper. I felt privileged to hear the stories of their accomplishments, disappointments, worries, abilities, strengths, and wishes, regrets and plans. They let me, a complete stranger, into their lives for and hour and shared a lot with me. So I want to share that with the world for them and their families.

Why a book on these older men? Because they have value. They have wisdom, they have learned lessons, worked hard, and have experienced so much. They can teach and direct and advise the younger generation. They can also gain complete satisfaction for a life well lived, and did the best they could with what they had. They can claim their strengths, forgive their enemies, family and friends and realize they are great. They can heal themselves and be proud of who they really are without any external identity labels. They are husbands, fathers, grandfathers, brothers, sons, friends and neighbors. They have so much to say, and I want to validate and acknowledge their value, sensitivity, intelligence, and manhood and humanity.

A Snapshot in Time

This book is a beginning, a start, a brief look at what a few good men, in a certain place, at a certain time in life, a certain time in history, had to say. But it could all change in a day, or next month, or next year.

Men's Point Of View

"The buzz phrase 'active adult community' fits well with your description but it hides the necessity of all of us to come to terms with the end-game of life we all are playing out. And, by the way, we are doing so without any support form the community for this final challenge."

-- from a 78-year-old retired educator.

"The flipside of the satisfied provider is that of a man having to care for his Alzheimer's/Dementia afflicted wife, then having to decide about placement in a home, etc. Imagine the conflict engendered by the provider role-playing husband confronted with the impossible task of caring for his wife having an irreparable disease."

-- from a 78-year-old retired educator.

CHAPTER 1

WHO ARE THESE MEN?

"A man has got to have a place to go in the morning and something to do..."

-- Ted, a 73-year-old self-employed gentleman.

This is a story about a group of men at a specific time in their lives and at a certain time in history living in a special place. They answered questions about their own lives and about several significant topics such as family, community, generations, men and women, and society.

This is about their stories of their own lives. There is a great need now in society and the world for their strong, sound, wisdom and advice based on their years of experience and problem solving. We need to hear from these men about their lives and learn from their wisdom.

This chapter is designed to introduce this interesting group of men to you. I will begin by giving you some information about them as a group and then introduce some of them individually

I was fortunate to interview 34 men ranging in age from their 40s to 90s, most being in their 60s and 70s. The two youngest men were in their 40s; one was the son of another interviewee and the other was the son of an acquaintance of mine. Two of the men were widowers, one was divorced and the rest were married. Three of the men had been married three times and nine had been married twice. Most had children and grandchildren living nearby. Nearly all were retired except for three who were still working at least part time and one who was working full time and was not ready to retire.

Asked about the most significant person or persons in their lives, most answered that their families were the most significant; 19 said that their wives were the most significant and seven said their parents were the most significant.

Ten of those interviewed were originally from California, 19 came from other states and four hailed from other countries. Their careers spanned just about every area you could think of including machinists, home builders, engineers, lawyers, teachers, salesmen, computer experts, historians, drivers, jewelers, librarians, artists, financial services, photography, dentistry and business owners.

Many of these men are achievers; all have worked hard all of their adult lives. Here are some individual examples (Please note that all of these names have been changed.):

Elliot, 77, is a retired lawyer who worked on a dictionary project for a large company and was co-author of a scientific paper.

Jack, 87, is an artist who has earned several awards for his artwork created for family and friends. He also has a great sense of humor: "I'm not old, I'm ancient," he says.

Daniel, 79, is a busy retiree who spends much of his time as a volunteer for a local charity that serves and helps people. In his retirement he now has time to write poetry and participate in other activities. He finds that journaling and poetry can be therapeutic.

Fred, 81, has won several awards for his work in the food business.

Louis, 85, says of retirement that there is not enough time to do it all. He turns out for many hobbies, still speaks at groups and stays working with selling ideas. And still has time to show up for family events.

Lee, 68, was forced to retire very early due to an accident. Although he has struggled with his illnesses and the extreme changes in his life, he has found a way to get through it and has a new perspective to take him forward.

These and the other men continue to make contributions in their retirement.

"I appreciate life so much more now that I see the problems other people have. Makes me grateful."

-- Michael, 72, retired civil engineer

Michael, 72, is a delightful retired civil engineer. He is married with a son and a daughter and four grandchildren, Michael is from a large family—he has four brothers and three sisters. He remembers well and admires time spent with his grandfather hearing about the history of his life. He still wants to hike the whole John Muir Trail someday. Proud of his son, and strong in his faith, he would like to see his family more often. When I asked him what he might want to be remembered for, he did not have an answer. His most cherished memory is the birth of his children.

Michael has been retired for several years and volunteers for different organizations. He is with Peer Counselors, Friendly Visitors and Handy Helpers—all of which work with seniors. He also leads a Memory Group for residents at a local assisted living facility. He is very family oriented, loves volunteering, and loves people. He sometimes thinks he is too sentimental and emotional. Michael says, "When I go to fix something they want me to stay longer and talk. Some even find things that need fixing just to have someone to talk to."

These men have each brought their accumulated wisdom, experience and strengths to this new phase of their lives.

"Writing is a joy, a release, a thrill, a gift. I love the creativity."

-- John, retired business owner

John, 76, a former business owner and teacher, is family focused and has been retired for six years. He took up writing as a joy and a release and is now a published writer and poet. He shows up regularly for many groups and activities.

Bill, 71, is a wonderful artist and a musician who plays as part of a local band. He is retired engineer and draftsman who moved to California many years ago from a place with very cold winters. He loves living here and loves entertaining people.

Earl, 74, discovered that retirement brought out his true calling in life—giving back and helping people through his work at the Red Cross and other organizations. Earl is a family man who loves history and reading too. A self-described problem solver, he is bothered by people who don't think for themselves and base their values on what society thinks.

Floyd, 64, was a restaurant owner and is now working in a new profession. He has an interest in music as a hobby and takes the time to share it in senior centers. He is not interested in retirement at this time as he feels he still has too much to do. He gets his strengths and determination from his faith in God.

Two of the men were far younger than most were facing the same challenges far earlier in their lives.

Gary, 42, is the son of one of the other men I interviewed. He is a stay-at-home dad for now and enjoying the time he gets to spend with his children. A former salesman, he is now coaching and teaching. He wants to be remembered for being a good Dad and is looking forward to his retirement.

Dennis, 44, has been living with a serious disability which is getting progressively worse. After several years at a job he loved—managing a high-tech group—he is unable to work now. Despite his challenges, he is a photographer and artist and he keeps busy using his creativity restoring old cars like his father has done. Dennis has put a lot of thought into life and is facing the future bravely. He hopes at some point to write a book about his life.

One common thread that ran through just about all of these men despite their very different backgrounds was a newfound feeling of freedom.

Retirement for these men has for most meant that for the first time in their adult lives they have freedom. They can be as active as they want to be or they can stay home and enjoy doing nothing. They can do exactly what they want to do. Retirement represents complete freedom and independence for them after years of working and handling family pressures.

These men, many for the first time now, have the time to explore new things as well as time to reflect on their lives and come to terms with any unfinished issues. They can make amends if needed, and realize they did the best they could in their lives. This process is really a life review process and in varying degrees is a natural life progression for just about everyone.

Not all men embrace this life review process, but those that do seem to be more at peace with themselves at a time in their lives when they should be at peace. I discuss the life review process in a later chapter and the most important thing to say here is that it is a process that needs encouragement and support and recognition from family and friends. It results in a very healthy self-reconciliation as well as an opportunity to tell one's story and leave a legacy for one's family and friends.

Of course, these men are not all happily retired. The story can be quite different if one is ill, disabled, does not have a good retirement income, or if one suddenly loses a loved one or becomes a caregiver for a spouse. The next chapters will look at these men and their stories both good and bad.

MEN'S POINT OF VIEW

"I am a unique individual and when I look at what I have it impacts me. I had no direction and have been a stone cast into the water and skipped and ended up in the right place at the right time. Karma, fate, luck or whatever, I've landed on my feet, not prepared for anything."

-- from a 67-year-old very busy retiree.

"In my whole life things just happened. No plans. I just plod ahead with the help of God and Jesus. I don't claim any strengths, just muddle along and things just work out."

-- from a 77-year-old retired lawyer

MEN'S POINT OF VIEW

"Retirement is the best opportunity to do whatever you want."

-- from a 73-year-old retired lawyer and engineer and now a very busy volunteer.

"I'm a go-to kind of guy. Want something done, call me."

-- from a 69-year-old, retired from industrial sales, who loves being involved, loves helping people get things accomplished.

CHAPTER 2

RETIREMENT: HAS ANYTHING REALLY CHANGED?

"I am no longer who I used to be, so what am I to do for the rest of my life?"

> -- Lee, 68, who found his way from losing his identity to a new way of looking at life.

Theoretically, retirement is supposed to be the time in one's life when a man can do whatever he wants—he is free from the daily demands of work and career.

Retirement can literally be a shock to the system—a dramatic, traumatic change in a person's life that can rank in severity and impact with divorce or the loss of a loved one. Depending on the individual and that person's level of preparedness for such a potentially dramatic change, the impact of that shock to the system can run the spectrum between positive to neutral to catastrophic.

The concept—and reality—of retirement affects different men in different ways.

Some men see it as the Holy Grail—the goal, the end game of what they have been working toward all of their lives. For others, retirement means that nothing changes. Some are still busy, still active, still working full time or even if that work involves a hobby, a part-time job or volunteer work.

For others, retirement can be a disorienting, depressing, even disabling experience.

For some men in particular, self worth and self esteem can be tightly tied to one's career and work achievements. For so many years, some men are so singularly focused on their job, that they do not develop the other parts of their lives. They have few friends outside of work and tend to not develop outside interests and hobbies.

When retirement finally comes, these men find that they quickly lose their identities—they really do not know who they are and what to do outside of going to work each day. It is a critical point in a man's life and will literally determine the course of his remaining years of life. Some embrace this opportunity and some shrink away from it.

Nearly all of the men I interviewed for this book live in the same retirement community, one filled with many opportunities to participate in classes, groups, and activities. I thought that talking about retirement in general and their decision to live in this retirement community would be good places to start.

How Is Retired Life? How Do You Like Living In This Community?

One of the most surprising things I discovered was that almost all of the men I interviewed said they were very happy being retired. It was as if they had worked all their lives just to do that. Finally, all of their work pressure is gone—no boss telling one what to do. They could sleep in as late as they wanted, and could finally take up the hobbies and things they never had the time to do. The other thing that became very obvious is that there is an abundance of things to do here to keep busy.

Some of the comments I heard included: "Great! Love it!" "Perfect, so many things to do." "Surprisingly fun." "Love it, the beginning of a new life…" "The best part of my life…"

To be fair, I want to again stress that this sampling of interviews really only represents the population in this one retirement community and not the population at large, most of these men have the financial resources to be comfortable and even considered wealthy compared to some others.

The Best and Worst?

Many more interesting comments came out when I asked the men what they thought the best and worst things were about retirement and about their situation.

Many said that they loved the community, the abundance of activities and the ease of meeting people but "missed seeing younger people around."

"There is a great range of activities but also a lot of sameness. The rigidity of codes is stifling and frustrating at times."

"It is orderly but so much the same."

"It is a beautiful area, good activities and quiet, but I felt like I was put out to pasture."

"There are many people with common interests; people are friendly, open, tranquil and educated, but not quaint as where I came from and there are more mosquitoes."

"There are beautiful programs that encourage social interaction, but maybe the rules are too restrictive."

One man said he and his wife had planned to move here from another state to be near their children. His wife died just before they were supposed to move; now he lives here alone. Another man said he chose this community especially so that his wife would have friends and support after he passed away.

One man said that he found retirement boring and felt that he "was just killing time."

Another is enjoying his retired life and has a great positive attitude about it all, despite receiving treatment for a serious disease.

One of the few men I interviewed who did not live in the retirement community is still working and not ready not looking forward to retiring. He still lives in a "mixed" neighborhood and would not want to live in a senior community. He said that he likes the mix of different people.

What Special Hobbies Do You Have?

This question brought responses covering just about anything one could imagine from such a diverse group: reading, dancing, golf, volleyball, woodworking, writing, painting, pool, music, fixing things, computer work, singing, fishing, restoring old cars, poker, genealogy, gardening, Toastmasters (public speaking), model airplanes, travel, brewing beer, politics, photography, bicycling, stamp and coin collecting, swimming and weight training.

Volunteering: A Significant Part Of Retirement

During their working years, many men do not have the time to participate in volunteer activities, other than perhaps coaching a sports team that their child happens to be a part of. In retirement, there is the time to pursue volunteering opportunities and it is a very popular activity among many of the men I interviewed. Volunteering not only helps others but it can also bring a sense of giving back and a sense of accomplishment.

One of the programs in our community here is a program staffed by volunteers called Neighbors Indeed. It provides information and referral services for the residents and their ongoing needs. They maintain lists of all the resources available in the area and help people access those services as their needs change as they get older. This service can also provide for the acquisition of medical equipment and a very popular Handy Helper program that provides residents assistance with some household chores like changing furnace filters, changing smoke alarm batteries, maintaining garage doors and even providing assistance with computers. Several of the men I interviewed volunteer for this program and are able to provide valuable assistance to fellow residents, while at the same time feeling good about their own lives and contribution.

The men I interviewed who live outside the retirement community are also active volunteers in their own neighborhoods.

Here are some brief stories from these giving, volunteering men:

Jack, 87, is a retired machinist. He has been married for more than 60 years and retired for 20 years. He is active in several groups including the Knights of Columbus, SIRS (Seniors In Retirement), Veterans Group, and at a museum in nearby Sacramento, Calif. He is also an artist and does woodworking.

Joshua, 69, married for many years, worked in sales in several cities, met many interesting and famous people in his work. In retirement, he is still very busy and shows up at several organizations in the city to help out whenever he can. Of retired life: "you have the best of everything with beautiful diverse people, where you can be as active as you want to be."

Samuel, 78, has done research and worked as a teacher in several places across the country. He contributes his expertise now as a volunteer for many activities and committees. He enjoys being active.

Duncan, 69, enjoys solving problems and is a "go-to" kind of guy. He worked in sales before his retirement and now is very active in helping and inspiring others.

The men interviewed who have found a peaceful transition into their retirement really seem to move on with their new lives in a positive and happy way. And for those whose path has led to volunteer work as part of that retirement have found a real-life application of the old saying "what goes around, comes around" in that many of the good deeds that they do for others will benefit them when they need help.

MEN'S POINT OF VIEW

"I love all the activities and friendship; as we get older the most important thing is having people around you."

-- from a 74-year-old retiree who had several different careers in the newspaper business, real estate and finance.

"I found out retirement was my calling. Now I'm giving back, helping people through organizations and groups."

-- from a 79-year-old very involved volunteer.

MEN'S POINT OF VIEW

"Ice and snow influenced my career change from bike messenger to draftsman."

-- from a 71-year-old retired engineer and draftsman

"Thinking things through is very important to me. I like it and enjoy doing it and I like to see it in others."

-- from a 78-year-old retired educator.

CHAPTER 3

HOW THESE MEN SEE THEMSELVES

"I am loving, honest, tenacious and hardheaded."

> --Douglas, 77, retired search and rescue worker.

As I have gone through this process of interviewing this group of men, I have quite honestly felt privileged to be able to sit down and talk with them about such a wide range of topics.

I had certain expectations about what they might have to say and really did expect their responses to my questions to be similar to one another. I have been very surprised by the diversity of and differences in our conversations.

Some of the men surprised me at how much they had to say—how open they were to answering my questions—while others were bordering on simple "yes" and "no" answers and were more reserved. One great example of this diversity and range of the responses was hearing some of the men say very definitively that their wives were the most significant people in their life. Others did not even mention their wives.

The questions I asked helped me to understand much about what they treasure, value and love; I also learned what they resent, regret and what they like to reminisce about.

We talked about what they believe are their strengths and their weaknesses. I asked them to tell me about their most embarrassing experiences and greatest examples of forgiveness. I found that many of these men do not talk about these things easily, especially when it comes to identifying and claiming their strengths.

One of the most fascinating areas of our conversations came when I asked what advice they had for young people, men and women, and what ideas they had to change or improve the world we live in, as most believe it is in very bad shape. That discussion comes in a later chapter.

Interestingly, it seemed to me that many of these men were talking out loud about many of these subjects for the first time—I could see many of them in deep thought as they struggled to put together their answers.

Here are some highlights of responses to my questions.

Favorite Thing, Person, or Time?

Responses to this very broad question were wide ranging: "family members," "sons," "wife," "mother," "grandmother," "the 1950s," "simpler, better times," "mornings," "Christmas," "travel," "the time after my divorce," "my time in the military," "a hot shower," "a good night's sleep," "my car."

Your Strengths?

In our conversations, this was not an easy area for the men. Many struggled with introspection and worked hard to really think about their answers, especially with regard to expressing what they felt were their strengths. Their strengths though modestly expressed are obvious to this interviewer.

Some examples: "enjoy people," "loyalty to family and country…" "love of nature," "ability to cope…" "determination," "success as a writer and a person…" "a serving attitude…" "tough," "no barriers," "takes responsibility for others…" "discovery and recovery…" "a little above-average IQ…" "ability to come back after being down…" "face fears," "power of reason and problem solver…" "stable," "very loving," "positive, focused…" "think things through," "honesty," "taking care of the little guy…" "help others," "good listener," "sensitive, perceptive…" "accept people for who they are…" "perseverance," "persistence," "the Lord living through me."

Fred, 81, an award-winning businessman while he was working, is enjoying his retirement now along with tournament poker and pool. He is involved with helping people through discovery and recovery and gains much strength through his participation in the Twelve Step Program.

Lee, 68, a very successful professional who taught others as well as launched a business was forced to retire early due to an accident. He looked inward for the strength he needed to go on, but has been able to turn his life around. He now volunteers in several activities.

Jesse, 80, used to work as a draftsman and designer. He moved to California from out of state to be near his family. He has many hobbies and is gifted with a talent for music, but now must call on his strength to face a serious illness

Words That Best Describe You?

I asked the men what words or phrases best described them whether it was a word that they might use or that someone else has used at some point in their lives.

Some examples: "average," "people's person," "jovial," "fun lover," "too emotional," "loopy," "rough," "nice guy," "like to laugh," "big and crazy," "outgoing and talkative," "friendly and stubborn," "energetic problem solver," "thoughtful," "intellectual," "loving and caring father," "positive," "leader," "go to guy," "punctual," "handsome and makes a good impression," "obstinate and gracious," "good advisor from a belief in God," "silly four-year-old," "optimistic and easy going," and "multitalented."

Jesse, 80, said "he is usually happy and usually honest."

Lee, 68, told me "I'm a friendly guy."

Ross, 67, worked for an airline before retiring and moving to the senior community. He is a very active person who enjoys having time for hobbies and all the different activities available to him. He told me that he is "handsome and makes a good first impression."

Douglas, 77, worked in search and rescue for many years. He was also an avid skydiver. He founded a sports league in his retirement community, and he told me that he is "loving, honest, tenacious and hardheaded."

What Are You Famous For or Known For?

This was not an easy area for the men to talk about. When I asked them what aspect or accomplishment that they were famous for or best known for, many were resistant to answer, thinking it their answers might be seen as boastful.

Some examples: "nothing," "music, art and shooting pool," "smart, organized and dependable," "help and follow through," "humor, sarcasm, advice and friendship," "helping," "wrote many books," "see a problem and fix it," "counted on for love and showing up," "helping kids," "photographer," "good manager," "advisor to his sons," "wife's rock," "a hall of famer," "can count on me," "accepting other people," "active and compassionate," outgoing and caring," and "dedicated."

Bob, 67, retired several years ago from a job in the transportation industry. He really enjoys the amenities in his community. He has many hobbies and has had time to reflect on his life. He explores and shares his interests in writing and photography. He told me that he is known for "being open and accepting of other people to make them feel comfortable," and that he "enjoys inviting them into his life."

Douglas, 77, and **Fred,** 81, told me that they are known for being good listeners.

What Keeps You Going When Things Get Tough?

This was another question that brought a wide range of responses. There were several interesting threads that ran through the responses. Many of the men clearly looked to their faith and spiritual beliefs to help them through tough times.

Some examples: "help of God and Jesus," "Catholic faith," "hobbies," "will power," "persistence," "wife and fishing," "just keep going," "no tough times," "enjoying what I do," "friends," "thinking through tough times with an intelligent approach," "a buddy," "put head down and keep working harder," "humor and action," "faith and encouraging wife," "good outlook," "laughing it off," "my partner and I kick it around," "this won't matter in a year so keep going," "have faith and an open mind," and "prayer."

Your Relationship With Your Father?

The relationship a man has with his father is one of the most critical and formative of any relationship in his life and can remain a strong influence even long after that father has passed on.

When I asked the men about their relationships with their fathers, it did not matter whether they felt that they had a good or bad relationship, they all seemed to respond very strongly one way or the other. There were no neutral responses.

I found that some of the men have had much difficulty with resolving things with their fathers, while others have had good relationships with them. Others have never been able to say what they wanted to say to them because by the time they realized that they wanted to say something their father had passed away. One thing for sure is that the relationship between father and son is vital, precious, and very significant and important to a boy and a man.

A few responses from the men I interviewed:

Michael, 72, said that "My dad passed away and I wasn't there. He retired and bought a ranch. He was ill but didn't complain."

Jack, 87, said that "Memories of my mother and father were not good. My father who was an alcoholic died and I didn't get to see him."

Robert, 65, said that "My father fished with me. So I am always trying to catch that big fish for Dad."

There does seem to be a desire in men that slowly surfaces as they get older to be at least understood if not appreciated by his family and especially within the father-son relationship. Many of the men I interviewed worked hard and long hours away from home and didn't get to spend time with their families. A great example of this can be found with the late Steve Jobs, founder of Apple Computer. In an article for *Time* magazine (October 17, 2011), biographer Walter Isaacson wrote this in the final paragraph of the article:

> "I asked [Jobs] the one question that was still puzzling me: Why had he been so eager, during close to 50 interviews and conversations [for his biography] over the course of two years, to open up so much for a book when he was usually so private? 'I wanted my kids to know me,' he said. 'I wasn't there for them and I wanted them to know why and to understand what I did.'"

Granted Steve Jobs was only 56 when he died, extremely busy and famous doing what he was meant to do but he still regretted the lack of time spent with his children and wanted them to understand and know him even after he had passed away.

MEN'S POINT OF VIEW

"I want to be remembered for being a good dad and I am looking forward to retirement."

-- from a 42-year-old former salesman who is now coaching and teaching. He is a stay-at-home-dad for now and enjoying it very much.

"My son and I are squared away now because of the Twelve Step program. You make amends to people you have hurt."

-- from a 67-year-old retired mechanic, who likes to help others, likes being with friends, and being in harmony.

CHAPTER 4

TELLING THEIR STORIES...
A LIFE REVIEW

"Telling our stories gives us the opportunity to talk through all of these life experiences with ourselves and move forward with the rest of our lives."

We all have a story to tell—it's our legacy for our family and for the world. Why is this important? Does it really matter whether we tell our stories or just keep them to ourselves? How will our lives or the lives of people around us be impacted whether we tell our stories or not?

I believe that people need to come to terms with their lives—with what they had to do to survive, with what they are not proud of as well as their great accomplishments. They need to put all of these life pieces into perspective and either make amends or claim them and realize they did the best they could at the time.

Your life story can be as simple or as complex as it needs to be. It can be about any and all of the experiences in your life that have shaped you and defined you as the person you are today.

When asked about their life stories, many people will focus on a single period or aspect of their lives—something really significant and life-changing such as a person's experience during wartime. And while wartime experiences are significant, they are not the only significant experiences in one's life.

All experiences—anything from the birth of a child to the death of a loved one; from a special place or time to a horrific one like a war experience—can shape us and leave lasting impressions, conflicts or celebrations unsaid. That's why telling our stories, at minimum to ourselves, is so important.

As we age, the cumulative effect of these good and bad experiences needs to be processed by each of us in our own way—things need to be reconciled and accepted for what they are. Each of us needs to have this self-acceptance to really be at peace with ourselves. Telling our stories gives us the opportunity to "talk through" all of these life experiences with ourselves and move forward with the rest of our lives.

Telling our stories to others gives us the opportunity to share a multitude of lessons learned and insight with those we care most about.

Think of the clarity that can come from exploring some of the big questions in our lives, especially in the lives of the older men in our families. Questions such as who did they hurt? Who did they help? What did they fail at? What did they accomplish? What did they say? What did they leave unsaid? What did they do badly? What did they do well? What can they claim is theirs alone? What makes them proud? What do they want their families and loved ones to know that has never been said?

Telling Stories Very Important For Men

As I have progressed with my thinking on the idea of life stories, I have come to the conclusion that there is a big difference between men and women in this area. I think that most women are more open and willing to embrace the good and bad of their lives and talk about them. Most men are not so open.

That's not a criticism. It's a statement about the overlay of expectations that society has placed on men—especially men of a certain age and generation—and that those men place on themselves. Strong and silent, take what life gives you, don't complain, and get up tomorrow to do it all over again.

I remember one of the things that really set me on this course to interview this group of men and help them tell their stories.

I was listening to the radio in the wee hours of the morning. The host was talking about a book, *No Average GIs* by Larry Colton, about three prisoners in World War II in Japan. It's truly hard to imagine how horrible a life experience that was for those three men and anyone who served in that war. The author was inspired to write his book because one of the three men had written a 20-page summary of his experiences. The two met and the author spent three days at his house interviewing him. Then an amazing thing happened. The older man died in the author's arms! The author took this as an incredible mandate to tell this man's story.

It spoke to me. It was another trigger that telling these stories was very important. So many of these men have stories—hidden deep inside—that reveal so many things: heroes, ideas, ideals, dreams, worries, fears, struggles, accomplishments, strengths, weaknesses, loves, hates, desires, hurts, and on and on.

Not all of the men I interviewed served in the military. There are many other hardships, making a living for a family, being a man, being tough, growing up, measuring up, living up to their own expectations and those of others, dealing with the changes in women, sexuality and society, and also many stories about just getting older.

There are others out there now working hard to tell the life stories of men.

The Veterans Organization here in our community of Lincoln has been working on a project, The Library of Congress Veteran's History Project, which is an outgrowth of the American Folk Life Project. Robert "Bob" Stackhouse and Doug Cooper have been working together for six years interviewing the veterans in the area. They make a video, send it to the Library of Congress for a permanent record and give a copy to the veteran. They have completed 80 interviews covering World War II, Korean and Vietnam war veterans. They find it very rewarding to the men, their families, and to the interviewers. They expect that the veterans of our more recent wars and conflicts will have a need to talk about their experiences in the future and hope the program can continue.

It is so important to get the stories remembered and told by these brave men who have for so many years put it completely out of their minds. They came home to families, went to work and supposedly forgot to remember this devastating and compelling experience. They were able to put it so far back in their minds that it was like it never happened. Some could not and had ongoing problems living with the memories. We really never completely forget and sometime later something could trigger the event and cause the flood gates to open up and they would be able to talk about it and work through the devastation. Then they could feel proud and relieved.

The late author and former newsman Tim Russert wrote a book about his father (*Big Russ and Me*) which was widely accepted and prompted many letters from readers telling him stories about their own fathers, and how proud of them they were. As a result of those letters, Russert wrote another book *Wisdom of Our Fathers* that tied those letters that he received together to tell stories about these fathers. Most of the men in Russert's book had already passed away and their stories were being told after their deaths.

In his book, *The Greatest Generation*, longtime news anchor Tom Brokaw wrote about men from that World War II era— mostly about men whose names you would recognize. On the other end of the spectrum is the excellent work by David Isay whose *Listening Is An Act Of Love* recounted life stories of people all across the country and from all walks of life.

Telling Life Stories One Way or Another

Writing life stories or memoirs has become a very popular activity at senior centers and senior communities. There was an article on this in the *Sacramento Bee* in July 2010 discussing this trend and observing that "the biggest reason for the upswing in interest is the widespread urge to let future generations understand that these lives amounted to more than merely names and dates on the family tree." The story was reporting on classes held at a community center in Sacramento where a group of seniors gather once a week to read the stories of their lives, sharing and preserving "many decades' worth of memories that would otherwise die with them." These groups are meeting in many other places and continue to grow in popularity.

The telling of one's life story with a goal of sharing it and also coming to grips with one's life is generally referred to as "life review." I spend Chapter 7 exploring the concept and process of life review in greater depth; the men I interviewed, whether they realized it or not, were in varying stages of life review.

As men get older and retire, they have the time to reflect on their lives. They remember and/or find out what they may have missed along the way due to individual circumstance, bad choices, in life's learning classroom. They may wish they would have done things differently but realize that life is just that—life. It is what it is.

If these men take enough time to really think about it, they will realize they did the best they could with what they had at the time. They will recall and remember anything unfinished or in need of amending and if possible they can amend it. Or they can realize they did what they did and now it's time to claim their strengths and the goodness of life, family, and friends and give back as they can.

What that says to me as the interviewer of these men is that by virtue of accepting my invitation to be interviewed, they have started their life review process. They are telling their stories to me. They can state what they have learned in life, teach others by their stories and advice, and benefit themselves by getting the acknowledgment they deserve.

Many Are Afraid to Tell Their Stories

The prospect of telling one's life story can be a painful, scary thing. Talking about one's life and in the process facing many things that perhaps one has not faced before can keep people from the life review process. It's for this reason that men, in particular, can leave so many things unsaid and unresolved.

Many families don't really know that much about their fathers—what they have done in their lives, how they feel about their lives—most men simply do not talk a lot about these things in their lives.

Men need to be encouraged to tell their stories, especially when they are older and retired. It's a time in their lives when they have the time to sort out their lives and make sense of them. According to psychologist Erik Erikson who wrote about the stages of psychological development in life, this stage is when we do a life review remembering what our life was about and having an opportunity to think about things. If there is something we have left unresolved we can resolve it, forgive if necessary, or realize we did the best we could with what we had and forget and move on. It is the time to take credit for and claim what we did in our lives. It is time to realize that we have a story to tell.

It can be a painful experience and that is why as family members or friends we should encourage this life review process. I met a man many years ago in a writing group who was writing about his experiences in war for his family and it was so painful he cried as he talked about it. But he worked through it. He needed to do it. It helped him finally sort out and come to grips with his life.

Why Are These Stories So Important?

These stories are important at the very least to their families—to let them know about their lives, the ups and downs, the good and bad, the strengths and weaknesses. The families and those closest to these men want to learn about their dreams and wants, the failures, the choices, bad or good and their struggles and successes.

Eugene, 78, is a very articulate and thoughtful person with a good moral compass, an engineer who and worked out of the United States for a while and learned to love the people and the country. But he came back here in California and now retired living near family and is enjoying it very much.

Don, 75, a retired civil engineer and family man, worked diligently with the local Grand Jury for a term, and now spends his time reading, working in the garden, and fixing things. He shows up whenever there is a need for problem solving and repair.

The stories are important to the men themselves—it's part of reconciling and becoming comfortable with their lives. This is the perfect time to do it—they have the time to look back examine, recall, remember, make sense of it, and correct any wrongs they can. They can forgive and forget and move on.

They can follow up on anything they have left undone and claim a life well lived.

William, 72, is dedicated to his marriage and family and also regularly volunteer doing computer work for an important project in Lincoln. Influenced by an uncle he describes as a self-made man with no education past the tenth grade who became a multimillionaire, he believes in always doing an honest day's work for honest pay.

Jerome, 69, is philosophical and interested in many different topics and activities. He is still employed part time and enjoys both retirement and working. He gives his time to volunteer and to also have time to get closer to God. He says he has accountability to God. The best of both worlds works for him.

Ben, 68, moved to California to be near family. A retired historian, he has worked mostly on the East Coast. He showed up here saying that retirement is the "best part of my life." He has liked getting involved in activities and social interactions. His hobbies include sharing his talent for music. He volunteers with an organization which helps others here in the community who need help to do things

These stories are important for society—everyone benefits from the lessons these men have learned. Society needs to hear their unique different point of view, advice to other men, women, the young, ideas to help the country, experience and wisdom in general.

George, 87, is a retired teacher and author, works on a historic project in a nearby town. Before that he wrote books about and taught foreign languages. He continued his writing and dedication when he wrote 10 books about the area.

Bert, 73, is a retired attorney and engineer who still works after retirement to continue doing deposition work for a water agency. He is also very involved in activities. He tells a story about the time an airplane crashed in Southern California. He was supposed to be on that plane but something came up and another colleague was supposed to go in his place. That colleague decided to take an earlier flight the night before and both missed what would have been a fatal flight. Wow!

In general, older people are put in the background just when they really know what life is all about. We need them out in the foreground with the rest of society to offer help reassurance, wisdom, confidence, and the knowledge that this too shall pass.

Some will need to have help telling their stories. Some will never go any further in telling their stories. Some will not want their stories known. Some do not believe they have a story to tell. They feel they are no more than ordinary men who lived their lives. That would be their story.

These men had plenty of great advice to share, and in the next chapter, I will share with you, what they had to say about the differences between men and women.

MEN'S POINT OF VIEW

"Church is important in our lives It can be great influence in young lives learning about giving and forgiving. My wife and I talk about our very good life and are waiting for the other shoe to drop. We don't deserve such a good life. My childhood is my greatest and best memory."

-- from a 71-year-old very humble, positive, retired home builder, who works with a group helping others in the community.

"About society he says that our faces turned backward away from God. People need to be less judgmental of each other. When wrong is done resolve and forgive bitterness."

-- from a 64-year-old quiet, not-yet-retired gentleman.

Men's Point Of View

"Love this woman like you want to get up from bed with her 50 years from now and treat her like Christ who loved the church treats you."

-- from a 79-year-old retired businessman, said to his grandson at his wedding.

"My wife changed my life for the better."

-- from a 77-year-old retired search and rescue worker.

CHAPTER 5

THOUGHTS ON THE DIFFERENCES BETWEEN MEN AND WOMEN

"Women compliment each other when they don't mean it and men insult each other because they like each other."

--Gerald, 86, a fun loving -retired gentleman.

Much has been written over many years documenting and attempting to discern the differences between men and women. Some would say that men and women are truly different species; others believe that environment and society make up for much of the differences.

The men I interviewed had a lot to say on this subject. Interestingly, while they found many differences—both subtle and obvious—most of what they had to say about women over their lives was positive.

Because there have been so many changes over the years with regard to women and their role in society, some of the older, more traditional men I interviewed have had more difficulty accepting those changes while others have seen and become more used to the many changes since women's liberation and have adapted to them in relationships and in the workplace. Divorce has become more prevalent, so some of the men have been married more than once.

Women have changed drastically since the 1960s and men have made some changes too. In the younger population more women are working. Right now due to economics and other factors, there have been many role reversals. Some men are having more trouble getting jobs than women and some end up being stay-at-home dads while the wives are working to support the family.

In my interviews, one of the sections of my questionnaire covered what they thought about women and the differences between men and women. Some even used the phrase "Men are from Mars and women are from Venus" to describe the depth of the differences. Here are some highlights of responses to my questions, grouped generally by the question I asked.

In General

Interestingly, two of the men interviewed saw no differences between men and women. Three men said that "women like shopping." Other comments: "women have a lack of self esteem but are really unique and beautiful;" "some women are trying too hard to be equal;" "women are sweeter;" "women are the more perfect of the two."

On Relationships

"Women compliment each other when they don't mean it;" "men insult each other because they like each other;" "women better attuned to personal relationships would make better spies;" "women are social and have friends, men are not social and don't have close friends and are lonelier;" "women are warmer and more considerate;" "women connect better and are good listeners;" "women are more insightful about human nature and are reliable."

On Emotions

"Women let emotions out;" "women are about feelings;" "men are more visual."

On Communication

"Women are talkers, men are doers;" two men said. "Women have better insights on how people relate." Three said "women are eager to talk;" "men are more direct;" "different reasoning between men and women."

On Problem Solving

"Women are smarter than men, they use their heads and hearts to solve problems;" "women are more organized;" "women are multitaskers; they juggle many tasks, men do it in serial order;" "more focused than men—they know what they want;" "women are higher achievers and more capable in particular jobs;" "more qualified in everything except physical labor; " "women more organized;" "women get things done while men talk about them" and by contrast one another man said "women are talkers men are doers."

What Advice Would You
Offer To Women?

Some examples of the advice the men would offer to women: "be proud;" "know your place 10 feet behind men;" "listen;" "if man is kind to you be kind to him;" "have confidence in yourself;" "shut up and learn;" "be true to your husband;" "recognize when the guy is really trying to make you happy and try to get on his side;" "don't buy into attitudes that work against you;" "forget what other people think of you;" "treat your husband well;" "if abused, get out if he hits you once;" "you have a lot of control sexually;" "encourage feminine side of men subtly;" "stress education;" "women can prove themselves to the world."

What Advice Would You
Offer To Other Men?

Some examples of the advice the men would offer to other men: "grow up;" "stand your ground don't get pushed around;" "speak up to women;" "love your wife and be true to her;" "treat women with more respect;" "find a good woman, love, listen, be patient;" "don't be so antisocial; life is full of discoveries;" "be true to your wife;" "be softer; try to put yourself in her place;" "listen carefully;" "be yourself;" "respect the woman you married;" "the more you give the more you get back;" "try to listen to your intuition;" "keep track of what women are doing, they are going to pass you by;" "be more honest in who you are."

Gerald, 86, is very much in love with his second wife, and has committed his time and talents to making the very best of the marriage.

Floyd, 64, offers, "Develop more understanding of the other—look into each other's eyes."

This author saw some differences between men and women too.

The biggest difference is how difficult it is for most men to open up, let their guards down and just be themselves. Women on the other hand are more open, more willing to tell you what's on their minds.

Is it all bravado? Do they speak the truth or just what they think you want to hear? I interviewed one gentleman and he answered all the questions I asked him briefly and tersely. I finished and turned off the recorder. Then he started talking. He told me about people he liked, famous people he met, how he met his wife, his favorite book, his favorite charity, how he got started and all in great detail, and with emotion and feelings and enthusiasm. The first half hour on tape was like taking a test or getting the work done so he could relax and be himself, which he was and was delightful, full of joy and fun. His eyes lit up and he was being himself and talking freely.

So what does that say to me and what does it say about the interviews?

I think that the men want to put it the way it should be put. They want to show themselves as on top of things, in charge, in control, as the husbands, providers, and fathers, they are with no flaws or fears or failures. There is another side—the struggles, hardships to overcome, strengths, regrets, wishes, and loves and passions. I want to see how they came to be the person they are now.

If I compare them to the women I interviewed I would say the women were more honest and forthcoming; men have to be macho and manly at an early age and it continues through their lives.

We women seek our authentic selves in many ways often by talking about it with other women. I have a sense that most men do not do the same thing. When do they seek or find their authentic selves? What is it for men to be authentic? Do they do it when they play golf, softball, pool or get together for coffee? Some get out and are involved in the community speaking, joining clubs, taking classes, running for office, serving on committees, but that is the minority. What about the majority? How do they find their authentic selves?

Aside from the differences I found in the interviews here are some words from a speaker at Stanford University I found online posted on "The Grateful Goddess Club" on February 8, 2011. The author wrote:

> "This was received by email and I was unable to confirm the author or the validity, but I would believe it to be true.

> **They Teach It At Stanford**

> I just finished taking an evening class at Stanford. The last lecture was on the mind-body connection—the relationship between stress and disease. The speaker (the head of psychiatry at Stanford) said, among other things, that one of the best things that a man could do for his health is to be married to a woman, whereas for a woman, one of the best

things she could do for her health was to nurture her relationships with her girlfriends.

Women share feelings whereas men often form relationships around activities. Men rarely sit down with a buddy and talk about how they feel about certain things or how their personal lives are going. Jobs? Yes. Sports? Yes. Cars? Yes. Fishing, hunting, golf? Yes. But their feelings? Rarely. "

Clearly, my interviews with the men have brought out some of the differences between men and women. Isn't it wonderful that we are different? We can complement one another, support one another, help one another, and love one another and accept and respect the differences that make life so interesting.

Men's Point Of View

"You young people are going to get old someday so have a talk with yourself. You are bulletproof before 40, and then you are vulnerable. Trust your gut then research it."

-- from a 67-year-old very busy retiree.

"Young people, be honest and do what you say you'll do. Work hard and don't give up when it gets tough. Stick to it. That's a good work ethic."

-- from an 87-year-old retired food business expert.

Chapter 6

Great Advice For The Younger Generations

"**Be very careful who your friends are, because you are known by your friends. Watch what you do. Things you do today may come back to bite you in future years.**"

-- Jesse, 80, a gentleman who has worked as a draftsman and designer.

Have you ever wondered what your father or grandfather would have to say about the younger generation today? Would he think that today's young people are very different than his generation? There have been so many changes that have resulted from the technological revolution. Your father grew up at a time when there were no cell phones, let alone iPads, iPods, YouTube, video games or even television (which also wasn't really around when he grew up); no Facebook, Twitter, Kindles or Nooks, and on and on. It really was a different world back then.

With this incredible revolution in terms of technology and information, we are constantly connected and inundated by new "anything goes" gadgets, ideas, tricks, scams, constant communication and multitasking. These fantastic innovations have also opened us up for a complete loss of privacy and in some cases, danger.

These continued leaps and bounds in technology bring changes everywhere. There is no denying it.

What about the older, experienced, wise person's point of view? In the midst of all of this change what do older men think about the changes around them? What do they think of the younger generations growing up in this radically different time?

I felt pretty confident that the older men would have a lot to say about the way things are now and how much things have changed over their lifetimes. I also thought that would have plenty of interesting advice for their families and society. Specifically I asked them two basic questions: What major differences do you see between your generation and today's youth; and what would you like to say to the younger generation?

These older fathers and grandfathers had some very interesting and wise things to say indeed. Here are some of their comments:

"Instant gratifications and being entitled is not written into the Bill of Rights or laws."

-- Ted, 73, who is still working in his own company.

"You're going to get old someday so have a talk with yourself. You are bulletproof before 40 then vulnerable."

-- Bob, 67, retired for several years after working in transportation.

"You have too many gadgets—we had none had to wait until we could afford to buy."

Several of the men had been married more than once and two of them offered these comments:

"If you are married, work through it not around it—don't divorce."

"If you are married, love your wife like you want to get up from bed with her 50 years from now; treat her like Christ treats you."

The differences they discussed were mainly in technology and the "gadgets" available to them. Other comments included that the younger generation doesn't really communicate because of the impersonal nature of the gadgets; they don't understand the risks. Some think today's youth are impatient and want it all now; that they have a sense of entitlement and a lack of discipline and manners; and that they have a bleak future.

One was worried about the broken homes some are in. Another said today's young were less bigoted and smarter and more open minded. A few said there were not many differences.

One was seeing mostly negative when he said, "They have no pride in their appearance, no attention span, no good penmanship, they don't write and can't make change."

Another of the men said, "They lack discipline and need it. The parents are spoiled brats raising spoiled brats."

Asked about what advice they would offer young people, most of their advice was about college, career, work, relationships, dreams, role models, taking time and the importance of spirituality.

"Please go to college and find a profession to help others in a meaningful way."

"Study hard and get a degree and be financially responsible."

"Always do an honest day's work for honest day's pay."

"Follow your dreams and find purpose not passion, passions change."

"Find a role model—learn from that person and see what they do right."

"Life is a long marathon, not a sprint."

"Get to know the Lord and find out His will for your life, and follow that."

The wisdom and experience of these men—who have been and there done that—is worth listening to. Much of what they had to say is positive and constructive and worth considering. These men have definite points of view. Their lessons can teach and help others. They can show up where needed to advise and lead.

Concerns About Society

Most of the men I interviewed had concerns about society and the way things are now. Being from a different time and a different generation they have seen many changes. They have more time to pay attention to what is going on. They sit back at a distance from the working society and can see the problems and changes.

Some of the topics that concerned them included politics, materialism, economics, immigration policies, moral decline, lack of civility, turning away from God, abuse of freedoms, government not meeting the needs of the people, and being disconnected from each other.

Their advice to help change it comes from their experience, what they had seen before, and expertise in many areas. Among some of the things that they said: "value relationships;" "education is key;" "politicians need to spend time in the classroom, change personally then carry [those changes] to local, state, and nation;" "get involved in volunteering," "change by being examples;" "keep at it;" "we all need to work together;" "look at yourself and are you doing what is worthwhile?"

They also said: "take care of your own and reach out to others and help;" "take care of the Earth and pollution;" "go back to old values;" "re-program with common sense;" "treat people with the Golden Rule;" "socialize more with family;" "church can be great influence;" "write to congressmen;" "be less judgmental."

This is all good advice but how do they (we) get that advice out there and get people to listen and pay attention? Here are a couple of ideas.

An article in the *Sacramento Bee* in August 2010, talks about a group of residents of a local community club who meet for coffee every morning to debate what and how they would give as advice in the newspaper advice columns. What a great activity for the older, wiser seniors. The article states that a study conducted by the University of California, San Diego confirms that the elderly really are wiser than younger people. Their brains have slowed down and so are more likely to think things through. They have wisdom and experience. They are good problem solvers. Unfortunately they don't have an opportunity to share this wisdom and experience and advice with the younger generation.

There is a program here in our community of Lincoln called "Schools," founded and operated by local residents Sandy Frame and Cindy Moore. The program enables many seniors to volunteer to work at the schools in the classrooms with students to help them when needed with schoolwork and encouragement and advice. There are now 170 volunteers involved. In surveys conducted regularly by the program on feedback from the volunteers and the schools, they have found that it is helpful raising test scores and has many other benefits. The intergenerational interaction is great for the children, teachers, and also for the volunteers.

Can we set up a group of men who wish to be available to talk to school groups, churches in person and even online on websites and blogs, and other places to help problem solve and offer support and relieve anxiety and distress of some of the community and families?

Why not?

MEN'S POINT OF VIEW

"There are so many differences between kids now and when I was a kid. I went to a parochial school, came home one day and Mom asked how school was that day. I said 'Sister slapped me' and then Mom slapped me on the back of the head. Mothers today are so defensive of their children"

-- from a 78-year-old retired industrial engineer

"Young people, my advice is, because the economy is so bad, the ability to make a satisfactory future is dim so I seriously suggest you leave and go to Canada. You have to find something that motivates you and it's hard to do in this economy."

-- from a 78-year-old retired teacher, now actively involved in community.

MEN'S POINT OF VIEW

"To fix problems in society, keep at it. It will improve if we all work together—it did before."

> -- from a 72-year-old computer operator, dedicated to family, who volunteers for special projects.

"In society there is a lack of togetherness- no goals, it's all about 'me.' We need to change it, and get people involved in volunteering. This is the responsibility of churches and parents not by preaching, but by pointing things out to people."

> -- from a 69-year-old very busy volunteer retired from work in sales.

CHAPTER 7

LIFE REVIEWS

"Retirement is the best part of my life."

-- Ben, 68, a retired historian from the East Coast.

What is Life Review? Depending on how one uses the term, life review can be both a general activity and a specific process. In general, life review refers to the process of looking back to the past and reviewing the activities in one's life in order to bring perspective to one's present life. Life review in general can also be used to describe activities such as story telling, oral history, guided autobiography, and life history interviewing.

Life review activities can occur in many ways and can be intentional or incidental, active or passive, organized or free-flowing, and individual or group. Life review can be the recollection of a single event all the way up to writing one's life story.

As I have thought more about the concept of life review and done more research on the subject, I have realized that most life review activities happen much later in life than I would have thought. The most common time for one to engage in life review activities whether formal or informal is when one is affected by a health crisis or disability. In the early retirement years one is so busy enjoying the freedom and participating in many new activities and hobbies that the concept of looking back and trying to make sense of one's life does not seem to be important or necessary. This is especially true when one lives in a resort-like retirement community like most of the men I interviewed.

As I discussed in depth in Chapter 4 regarding telling one's stories, I also believe that men are less naturally disposed to undertake a life review process—they do not generally enjoy spending time talking about life issues. Women are much more open to this kind of exploration and would, I think, be much more likely to participate knowingly in a life review process.

Life review can be typically something one does in a crisis or after a loss—a personal tragedy, a divorce, or other life changing experience. As I noted above, the complete process involves looking back at one's life remembering the good and the bad, trying to make amends if possible, forgiving others and oneself, and acknowledging that one had done the best one could at the time. It's an involved process; often painful and emotionally draining. It's often time consuming.

The interviews I conducted with the men in this book are a form of life review, or at least the beginning of the process.

A Sudden Loss

Barney, 60, is still actively working. He is recently widowed and has family nearby. He is involved in local activities. He believes he can make a difference in his work. His Christian faith guides his life. He feels he is part of the problem and wants learn more so that he can be part of the solution.

A Forced Life Review

Dennis, 44, is a younger man who has been living with a serious disability that is getting progressively worse. He is unable to work now after several years at a job he loved. He is a photographer and artist and he keeps busy using his creativity to design a car as well as restoring old cars like his father has done. He has put a lot of thought into his life and is facing the future bravely. He hopes to write a book about his life.

Life review activities are quite common in nursing homes and other senior care facilities. They can be organized activities in these facilities that older people adjust to aging and the losses and problems of old age. It can help an older person to talk about some of the things that bother them or have hurt them as they remember their lives.

I really believe that one of the best times to begin a life review is at the beginning of one's retirement from work. This is a time when a person finally has the time to start to reflect— perhaps for the first time—on one's life to date. This can also be the beginning of an entirely new time of discoveries, new interests, new activities, new ideas, new friends, and new opportunities for continued growth and development.

Contrary to popular opinion, older persons do not quit growing and developing. Life after retirement is not all necessarily downhill. It is different than the driving force present in earlier stages of development but there is still development, according to psychologist Erik Erikson and his wife Joan Erikson, from their book *The Life Cycle Completed.* In fact, Joan Erikson has added a ninth stage of development to her husband's eight "Stages of Psychosocial Development." That ninth stage is "Older Age" because as she writes, "old age in one's 80s and 90s brings with it new demands, reevaluations, and daily difficulties. These concerns can only be adequately discussed, and confronted, by designating a new ninth stage to clarify the challenges." For more information on the Eriksons' work, please consult the aforementioned book.

In addition, David Solie contends in his book *How To Say It To Seniors* that it is not only natural for there to be reflection and looking back going on but it is necessary to the continued development of the senior. It is a person's task at this particular time in life in order to be able to "resolve the conflict between integrity and despair." Further, Solie says life review is going on whether one is conscious of it or not, and that such life review needs to be supported and encouraged to help the senior to be able to accept his or her life and pass on the legacy to the family and the world. He believes that life review can also improve communication between the generations.

So in this lovely retirement community here there is life review going on at many different levels and ages and it affects the lives of the retired men I interviewed in several ways even though it may be mostly unconscious and unacknowledged or just not discussed.

Didn't Expect To Be Alone

Ethan, 87, worked for many years in the food business, retired and came to this community to be near family. But his wife died just before he moved here. He is a widower who likes retirement but participates in just a few of the activities here. He showed up to be near and interact with his family He did not expect to do it alone.

Persistent Memories

Alex, 74, is retired but still a consultant in the field of computer software. He is a family man who enjoys the activities and finds them surprisingly fun. A very significant event in his life eventually led him to recall the memories of it and explore it further. He put it all together in a book.

Author David Solie reports that the reason it is important to know about life review is that it helps to explain some of the communication problems between the generations. If a person is torn between trying to maintain control over his life and also letting go of certain driving forces it may be difficult to communicate. He may be having memories that keep popping up and interfering with his taking care of business. Family needs to recognize when it is important to encourage discussion and thereby helping the senior to resolve some issues. It is important to listen.

I believe it works a bit like programs such as Alcoholics Anonymous (AA) where a person must go through several steps to turn his or her life around. For example, one of the men I interviewed was an alcoholic and had been involved in AA for many years. He claimed he had been able to influence the life of a close relative by talking about his mistakes and making amends to her and others he had hurt when he was actively drinking.

So you think when you retire your job is over? Let me tell you it is not. You have another job to do. That job is to make sense of your life and determine what you want to be remembered for and what you want to pass on to your family and society.

As mentioned before, psychologist Erik Erikson said that we have eight developmental stages in our lives. At each stage we have tasks to do and conflicts to resolve before we can move on to the next stage. For example the first stage is when a baby has to resolve trust vs. mistrust issues—with the outcome being hope. In adolescence we have to work out identity issues, in middle adulthood it is procreation vs. stagnation with the outcome being parenting and maturity. When one is over 65 years of age, the conflict is integrity vs. despair and the outcome is acceptance of one's life and wisdom to be passed on and shared with others.

The point is that this stage in life is another step. We seniors are still growing and developing.

The beautiful part of retirement is that we are no longer driven by the same forces that adult children are. We are not having to move up in our jobs, raise a family, keep up with the Joneses, launch our kids into college or careers, worry about when and how and where to retire. We have some time finally to spend on reflecting on life—time to smell the roses and the bacon and read a whole book or take up a new hobby or take dance classes as well as spend time with our grandchildren.

Everyone over 65 is somewhere in the process of life review whether consciously or unconsciously. In many different degrees we are looking back at our lives and reliving events and situations and relationships and trying to have them fit into what we value and went our lives to mean.

We are remembering what we did in our life and claiming it and accepting it as a good job, whether it's a career or raising a family, or other accomplishments. We need to give ourselves credit for what we have done in our lives.

There may be an incident where we hurt someone or someone hurt us and we reacted and broke or ended the relationship. When we look back we see that we overreacted and think we could have acted differently. Or that it was completely justified. So we may be able to file that incident away knowing we did the best we could have. Or we may want to contact the person and apologize. Either way we are doing life review and making sense out of our lives. After consideration, we need to know that we did the best we could with what we had. And we need to forgive ourselves and others for mistakes and move on.

Harold, 71, is very positive and always smiling. He worked as a home builder before retiring and is enjoying retirement very much. He is now leading others to volunteer to help people who need it and is now looking forward to travel. He has always volunteered to give back because he felt so blessed in his faith.

Ben, 68, moved to California to be near family. A retired historian he has worked mostly on the East Coast. He says that retirement is the "best part of my life." He has liked getting involved in activities and social interactions. His hobbies include sharing his talent for music. He volunteers with an organization which helps get things done for people in the community who need help.

The important thing to know is that we—older persons—do this universal life review, whether we know it or not. We are trying to make sense of the incident in the story about Uncle Albert, or Aunt Minnie or Mom or Dad or our spouse, and the way they acted and the way we reacted, or the bosses we had to deal with or the incident with the neighbors, etc. so we can put it to rest and move on. It is important to resolve these issues so we won't be bitter and in despair.

Family and friends can help a person by listening to the story and asking questions to allow the person to finish it and also by looking for the values the person is trying to glean from it. There are other clues to look for and other questions to ask to facilitate the process.

The point is that we all have a legacy to fulfill and the leave for our loved ones and the world. What is it you want to be remembered for? What do you want your family to know and remember about you?

MEN'S POINT OF VIEW

"Christian faith is the answer in terms of understanding loving God and loving people, if we consider others higher than ourselves would make a significant difference. The definition of love is choosing for the other person's highest good."

-- from a 60-year-old busy not-yet-retired gentleman.

"Had an event over 50 years ago and it took 25 years to recognize it. I knew I wasn't crazy but thought I was and was afraid to talk about it. It was something that would never leave me. I now talk about the memories and how they affected me. It is being put in a book."

-- from a retired marketing director of a software company.

MEN'S POINT OF VIEW

"The more you know about yourself, the more you know how far you fell from grace. This is a level of enlightenment. It's an interesting quest negative and positive because you get a more universal perspective on you and how you relate to society and life and how you are just a blade of grass blowing in the wind and then you are gone. I have accountability to God that's my primary accountability. He tickles the spirit inside of me. I am a practical perfectionist. Have to let it go."

-- from a 69-year-old semi-retired co-owner of a business.

CHAPTER 8

OFF THE CUFF: ANSWERS TO SOME LINGERING QUESTIONS

"Everything fell apart and then everything came together."

-- Ted, 73, on a particularly bad time in his life.

The term "off the cuff" means improvised, spontaneous or off-handed and came from the practice of men around the end of the 19th century who were about to address a group. They would use the stiff disposable cuffs of their formal white dress shirts as improvised note pads at formal dinners. Remarks needed to be brief to fit on the cuff.

As part of my interview process, I wanted to solicit some spontaneous, off the cuff answers from the men I interviewed. This part of the interview came after many questions that helped me to get to know each person. In the off the cuff section I insisted the men say the first thing that came to mind and try to keep their answers to just a few words.

This was not so easy for many of the men. They naturally wanted to think about what they wanted to say and say it just right. I was hoping that this section would provide truly honest answers without filters on their thinking.

I am treating the answers the men gave me in general topics and without attribution. I believe that these off the cuff responses probably triggered some more thinking—and hopefully some resolution—on regrets, resentments, struggles, forgiveness, unfinished topics, and reminded them of all they have to be proud of and grateful for and take credit for living a good life

Below are some of the highlights of the off the cuff answers.

Regrets: "Dad was killed by a car and I didn't see him before he died;" "not talking to kids more;" "not finishing college;" "not being nice to wife;" "crisis with brother;" "not enough time with parents;" "lost wife too soon;" "not being a better husband."

Struggles: "Family problems," "shyness," "sexual feelings," "weight," "financial," "controlling emotions," "disabled child," "self-image," "poverty," "following orders," "meeting people," "confidence," "lack of education," "loneliness."

Resented: "Easy success," "men who abuse children," "wives and animals," "people who don't care," "inconsideration," "prejudice," "selfish people," "arrogant pompous people," "stubbornness," "ignorance," "hypocrites," "liars," "politicians," "bigotry," "liberalism," "myself."

Left unfinished: "lots," "relations with children," "relation with my Creator," "reading books," "my life," "nothing."

Still trying to work out: "letting things pile up," "how system works," "relations with wife," "how to be more productive," "support when I am old," "nervous when I speak," "acceptance of people who violated me," "understanding women."

Need to forgive: "wife," "grandmother," "daughter-in-law," "myself," "older brother," "family," "parents," "sister in law," "no one," "God."

Never forget: "family," "wife," "fantastic childhood," "a teacher," "childhood friend."

Hardest thing you had to do: "unemployment," "forgive self," "taking tests," "apologizing," "bury first wife," "fire someone," "quit smoking," "divorce," "asking the Lord to forgive me."

Men's role of provider and protector: This is the role we have given the men in our lives and so it was interesting to hear what they thought about it. Most thought it was a good feeling but some found it to be difficult and a burden.

How does it feel to be responsible? "Good," "satisfaction," "difficult," "feels normal," "necessary burden, happy to do it," "big responsibility overvalued," "privilege and honor," "wonderful," "inadequate," "very rewarding."

What do you love? "Life," "sports," "art and music," "nap," "people," "wife," "good food," "sunset," "fun activities," "financial security," "family," "outdoors," "travel," "freedom to do what I want."

What makes you sad? "Bad situations," "when I see love," "screw up by me," "being alone," "sad movies," "sentimental things," "disasters," "animals abandoned," "kids hurt," "death," "seeing things unfold that wouldn't have happened had people been responsible," "awfulness of the world today," "books," "loss," "suffering," "injustice," "unfulfilled expectations."

Bucket list: One third of the men said that they wanted to travel and attend a high school reunion; some said that they should make a bucket list and a third of the men said that they had no bucket list.

Sports: While sports was not a big part of their lives anymore, most of the men saw sports mostly as entertainment, though some mentioned specifics like fishing, swimming, hiking, tennis and softball.

Current events: In this section I asked the men about some of the controversial topics of today.

Gay people: A small number were against the gay lifestyle, most were okay with it. Several said that they had good friends or relatives who were gay.

Abortion: One third had no problem with it, one third was neutral and one third was against it.

Immigration: Most thought that the issue needs a lot of work and a review of policy; a few thought that persons here illegally should be sent home. Some thought they should have the opportunity to become legal.

Women in the military: Almost all thought this was okay. Only a few thought it was not a good idea.

It Makes You Stronger…

These are strength building situations or problems that may have influenced the men and they overcame them to be stronger.

Elliot, 77, found that shyness was the biggest obstacle. He overcame it through the years, took speech class and "kissed the Blarney Stone." He then became a teacher and later a lawyer.

Michael, 72, was living away from his family which was difficult enough and then his father passed away while he wasn't there. He works with seniors and spends time helping whenever he can.

Don, 75, had to spend some time in a boarding school away from his family due to pressures of the time and his parents working.

Fred, 81, had to recover from bad choices he made. He overcame bitterness and a judgmental attitude with help from a friend who helped change his path.

Robert, 65, had major depression in his life but overcame it and excelled.

William, 72, regrets that he lost his father when very young but had the love and help of a favorite uncle in growing up.

Bill, 71, still struggles after he lost his mother at a young age, and then survived polio.

Fred, 81, had some rough times and got some inspiration from a particular quote from Winston Churchill: "If you're going through hell, keep going."

William, 72, witnessed a murder as a young child and couldn't speak after that, but with determination was able to regain his speech.

Barney, 60, lost his wife of many years to cancer.

Alex, 74, had a near-death experience as a teenager which he had repressed until he became an adult and then recalled the memories, and wrote a book about the incredible experience.

Daniel, 79, is working out his relations with spouse.

Ted, 73, is working out his relations with his children.

My hope in this part of the interview was to get the persons to maybe be reminded of things that they could still deal with, or make amends for, and to forgive others for hurting them, and forgive themselves for or get rid of any guilt about parts of their lives they regretted, and or accept the fact that they had done all they could do.

Finally, I wanted them to look at their lives and accept the fact that they had done the best they could at the time and now they could take pride in a life well lived. In essence, I wanted each of these men to begin their own life review.

MEN'S POINT OF VIEW

69

"Discovery and recovery. In the last five years I've learned more than I have for my whole life."

-- from an 81-year-old man, retired from an award-winning career in the food business.

MEN'S POINT OF VIEW

"I don't want to be in a nursing home, I want to pull the plug myself."

-- from a 65-year-old retired systems analyst.

"I'm in Purgatory trying to get from point A to point B but now stuck. Getting used to illness—and that I will decline until the day I die. Hard to adjust to that."

-- from a 44-year-old man facing a serious illness.

CHAPTER 9

THE OTHER SIDE
OF THE ROSY STORY

"The nearly constant presence of the ambulances and fire trucks makes us all think about whether they will be pulling up at our own doorstep soon."

As I finished my conversations with the 34 men I interviewed here in Lincoln, I could not help but conclude that they were happily retired and enjoying what they are doing. So what was I missing? Could they all be that happy?

I was struck that there did not seem to be a downside to their life experiences. I really did not find the loneliness and despair I found when I interviewed the 100 older women for my previous book. I had to ask myself if the men told me the truth or did they tell me what they thought I wanted to hear? Were their answers what they wanted me to hear, and either denying or just not sharing the negative side of their life experiences?

Because, of course, we know that there is always another side to the rosy story.

In looking more closely at the interviews, I saw that there were problems and issues they all had in one area or another. Certain of these things came out in the "Off The Cuff" section I covered in Chapter 8, so I knew that everyone was not completely happy and problem free.

However, I think that the biggest elephant in the room was one that almost no one mentioned to me: facing their own mortality.

A few times a week here in Lincoln, California, in this wonderful resort-like utopia we live in, there is the familiar sound of the siren—the notification that someone here is in need of assistance. The fire engine and ambulance are regular visitors up here. In fact, one often sees an ambulance sitting at the entrance of the community waiting for the inevitable call.

The nearly constant presence of the ambulances and fire trucks makes us all think about whether they will be pulling up at our own doorstep soon.

Why? Because we are of an age when things go wrong, things happen, one can have a heart attack, stroke, or a bad fall and then things can go from a rosy story to disaster in a moment. This entails one's life changing from actively involved in many different things to spending some time incapacitated and in need of a caregiver. This is a sudden change and happens all the time. This is the side we do not talk about. This is the trunk and tusks—part of the elephant in the room.

The other part of the elephant in the room that we don't see right away is something very significant. We don't want to see or acknowledge this, or talk about or allow it into our thoughts. What is it that we are avoiding?

Those of us who live here do not want to face that we are in the last act of the stage play called Life. We are into the final episode. We are facing the end—the finale. Even though life expectancy has increased we are running out of time. This flies in the face of our belief that we of the Silent Generation and Baby Boomers do not age or retire or die. And if we do not mention or think about it, then it will not happen, right?

As a community this eventuality is not faced directly here except for a very few presentations and speakers. That is understandable as the community is changing as people leave and others need to be attracted to the area. This is done with the multitude of activities available and the beauty of the neighborhoods and facilities.

While there are many happily retired people who come here to enjoy this time of life, there are many who are in a different place. They may be disabled, unhealthy, or in emotional pain, or may have been alienated from families, or had a really sad life. This is where it all comes together. You see the point is that even if one is involved there is still time to think about the things that have affected one's life. What would be of use to those who are not so "happy" at this particular time?

That is the big question, and it needs to be addressed, because of the possibility of sudden change in this age group and/or the natural, inevitable, gradual aging that takes place. We could have support groups to talk about such things. We could have and do have some writing groups to encourage memoir writing and life story writing. We could have more case managers, social workers and nurses available for consultation to provide guidance and resources for persons starting to have health problems and their families.

I've said before that the men I interviewed here in Lincoln Hills seem to be mostly pretty happy. They seem to be doing the things they want to do, when they want to do them, and they say they really like living here in this lovely senior community. They were all pretty healthy too.

Those other sides of the rosy issues that seniors have in their lives are true across the board in all other communities as well as here in this place. They can be all the negatives of natural aging plus any other disabilities or illnesses that happen that change from a healthy normal aging life to many losses of friends and loved ones, loss of control, need for a caregiver, disability, and perhaps even death. It doesn't seem to be talked about much here in this vibrant living community. Who wants to talk about it anyway beyond making sure one has worked out the end of life issues, financial, burial, wills, and made arrangements for finalities. There is so much more living to do. And there are developmental issues still going on for the senior.

In his book *How To Say It To Seniors*, David Solie makes a statement that really resonates with me: "That mission [the seniors' mission] is not to come to terms with their impending death, but to make sense of life." Solie's book is about the necessary task of older adults to do a review of their life, make sense of it, and come to terms with it, so they can leave a legacy to their families and to the world. He talks about good ways to encourage and support seniors in this task.

He believes, as does psychologist Erik Erikson, in the idea that there are development tasks to accomplish ongoing into our senior years. Solie also states the following:

> "Part of the myth we buy into about the aging process is that biology is destiny and determines everything the older person can do, feel, and think. We assume that outside of biological issues, there isn't much else to say about this age group. But once we get clued in to an elderly person's developmental agenda, we realize they are less concerned with biology than they are with maintaining the control they need to fulfill their mission. That mission is not to come to terms with their impending death, but to make sense of life."

This can be done by beginning the life review process. It is what goes on consciously or not, as the senior enjoys the activities available to them or not. Some are not as active as others but the life review still goes on. The idea of making sense of their life is reasonable—one has to believe that his life has had meaning and that he was here for something. So it's a matter of talking about it to others especially family and friends, and accepting theirs as a good life. Not doing so can lead to much bitterness and despair.

The men I interviewed for this book have worked hard all of their lives and need this peace of mind. I hope that I have helped them to begin their life reviews and would encourage you to help those in your life.

Because given the choice, I would like to choose the rosy side of life.

MEN'S POINT OF VIEW

"In society now we are disconnected from each other forced to be choices don't want to make."

-- from a 75-year-old retired engineer

Chapter 10

Name Your Own
Life Story

There is something very special about every one of the men I interviewed. I wanted to be sure to capture as much of the interesting life details I could about each of them. You have seen pieces of these men in previous chapters. I have changed all the names to protect their privacy and sometimes "generalized" individual comments, but I wanted to make sure I was able to find a way to express who each of these men are.

The last question in the interview was for each of the men to tell me what the title of a book about their life would be. They each gave me a title and I have listed them below.

Before I show you their titles, there was a section in the book *Seven Sacred Attitudes*, by Erica Ross-Krieger that reminded me of the men I have interviewed and inspired me to look at each individual and what he does. In the chapter about her "Sacred Attitude #5: Show Up," Ross-Krieger quotes an author and writes the following:

"In her book, *The Four-Fold Way*, cultural anthropologist, author, and educator Angeles Arrien, PhD, writes, 'Every human being carries the power of presence…Many indigenous societies recognize this capacity, often referred to as showing up or choosing to be present and visible. The power of presence means we are able to bring all four intelligences forward: mental, emotional, spiritual and physical…' When we choose to show up energetically, with all four intelligences, we express the power of presence."

Ross-Krieger says further that, "When we show up in the world—just as we are—and give voice to what matters most to us, magic happens." She gives examples of people she knows who have decided to make changes that changed their lives.

With the men I have interviewed here in Lincoln I found that several have done just that. In retirement, they find that they have the time to do exactly what they want to do. They can stay home and relax or they can take up dreams and act on them or they can volunteer, or travel. I found that these men have decided to show up and participate in something above and beyond their working expertise and have found ways to be themselves and do something individual to them and best for the community.

Here are some great examples of showing up. Below are the titles that the men I interviewed have chosen for the stories of their lives.

"Joe Average"

Elliot, 77, is a retired lawyer who worked for the state, participates in several activities here, travels with his wife, and takes the time to show up and care for and help out an older disabled relative in an assisted living facility.

"Peoples' Person"

Michael, 72, is a retired civil engineer and shows up to gives his time to be a Peer Counselor, Friendly Visitor and a Handy Helper, all who work with seniors.

"Fun Loving"

Gerald, 86, is very much in love with his second wife, and has committed his time and talents to making the very best of the marriage. He shows up with his wife and they participate in many groups and classes. They have a great time.

"Keeping Busy"

Jack, 87, has been married for more than 60 years, worked as a machinist. He has been retired for 20 years and is active in several groups and regularly shows up for Knights of Columbus, Veterans Group, SIRS, and is a docent for a museum in Sacramento. He is also an artist and does woodworking.

"Just A Bump In The Road"

John, 76, is a former airline employee, business owner and teacher, family oriented and retired for six years. He took up writing as a joy and a thrill and is now a published writer and poet. He shows up regularly for many groups and activities.

"Variations"

Bill, 71, is a wonderful artist and musician plays and instrument with a local band. He is a retired engineer and draftsman. He loves living here and shows up for special performances with the band to entertain people.

"Just When You Think You've Got It Made, Sh*t Happens"

Don, 75, is a retired civil engineer, showed up for the Grand Jury for a term, who now spends his time reading, working in the garden, and fixing things. He shows up whenever there is a need for problem solving and repair.

"Book Of Life: Finish Nice"

Daniel, 79, is an active retiree who spends much of his time showing up to volunteer at a local charity that serves and helps people. He is retired from library work, where he spent many hours working on studies that he sold to a medical association. He now has time to write poetry. He finds that journaling and poetry can be therapy.

"He Is A Caring, Loving, Committed Person"

Robert, 65, is a retired computer programmer and systems analyst who married his childhood sweetheart. He is showing up at a fishing club, chorus and his church. He loves the outdoors and especially fishing.

"I Still Haven't Grown Up, But I Am Trying"

Joshua, 69, moved here with his wife eight years ago. He worked in auto sales and now works in many different areas and endeavors. He shows up at several organizations and does them proud. He supports the library, Lincoln Kids, festivals, and even finds time to play softball.

"It's A Good Life, What's Next"

Ted, 73, is not retired; he is a self-employed investment manager is very involved in the community. He still finds time for golf and works on restoring a historic sports car. He shows up at community meetings and events too.

"WOW"

Fred, 81, is retired from an award-winning career in business. He enjoys tournament poker and pool, and he still shows up at AA meetings and is involved with helping people through discovery and recovery.

"He Did It His Way"

George, 87, is a retired teacher and author who started and now works on a historic project here in Lincoln. Before that he taught and authored books on foreign language. He showed up to write 10 books about this area!

"We Can Do It, The We Team"

William, 72, is dedicated to his marriage and family and shows up regularly, volunteers doing computer work for an important project in Lincoln. He was influenced by an uncle he describes as a self made man with no education past the tenth grade who became a multimillionaire, he believes in always doing an honest day's work for honest pay.

"It's Not Armageddon Yet & Being A Dad"

Louis, 85, says of retirement that there is not enough time to do it all. He shows up for many hobbies, still speaks at groups and works with selling ideas. And still has time to show up for family events.

"Learning Life's Lessons"

Earl, 74, found out that "retirement was my calling" and gives back helping people at the Red Cross and family counseling. He shows up for many activities, groups, and friends. He loves history, and reading too. A self-described problem solver, he is bothered by people who don't think for themselves and base their values on what society thinks.

"I Did My Best"

Lee, 68, worked at his profession, taught, and set up a business and then was forced to retire early due to an accident. He has found a place here in Lincoln Hills where he shows up and volunteers as well as enjoys his neighbors. He has found a way through depression and feeling like he lost his identity and has a new way of looking at life.

"Waking Up To Live My Real Life"

Gary, 42, is the son of one of the residents here. He shows up for his family. He is a stay-at-home-dad for now enjoying it very much as he can spend time with his children. A former salesman he is now coaching and teaching. He wants to be remembered for being a good dad and is looking forward to retirement.

"Born Lucky"

Bert, 73, is an attorney and an engineer. He shows up after retirement to continue doing his deposition work for a water agency. He is also very involved in activities. His book title came from the fact that a plane he was supposed to be on crashed in San Diego. Wow!

"A Rational Life"

Samuel, 78, is a professional in the field of psychology did research in visual perception and has worked as a teacher in several parts of the country. He contributes his expertise when he shows up here in the community for many activities and committees. He enjoys being active.

"Like The Good Old Days Or It Is A Good Trip?"

Duncan, 69, enjoys solving problems and is a go to kind of guy. He worked in industrial sales before retiring and has shown up here to be very active and involved in helping others. He enjoys working with several groups and loves his retirement. He is also very inspiring to others.

"Are You Ready For This?"

Ross, 67, worked for an airline before retiring and moving to this community. A very active person who enjoys having time for hobbies likes all the different activities here. But he finds time to show up to volunteer for an organization that works with children and horses.

"My Life"

Ethan, 87, worked for many years in the food business, retired and came to this community to be near his family. His wife died just before they were to move here. He is a widower who likes retirement but participates in just a few of the activities here. He showed up to be near and interact with his family.

"Give It Your All"

Eugene, 78, is a very articulate and thoughtful person with a good moral compass. He is an engineer who showed up and worked outside the United States for a while and learned to love the people and the country. But he showed up back here in California and now retired living near family and is enjoying it very much.

"Pearls I Have Gleaned From Life"

Jerome, 69, is philosophical and interested in many different topics and activities. He is still employed part time and enjoys both retirement and working. He shows up to give his time to volunteer and to also have time to get closer to God. The best of both worlds works for him.

"The Reluctant Return"

Alex, 74, is retired but still a consultant in the field of computer software. He is a family man who enjoys the activities and finds them surprisingly fun. A very significant event in his life eventually led him to recall the memories of it and explore it further. He showed up and put it all together in a book.

"A Sheltered Life, A Fulfilling Life: All Positive Experiences And Be Grateful For What You Have"

Harold, 71, is positive and always smiling. He worked as a home builder before retiring and is enjoying retirement very much. He shows up now leading others to volunteer to help people who need it and is now looking forward to travel. He has always volunteered to give back because he feels so blessed.

"Grandpa's Story: He Wrote About Life"

Jesse, 80, used to work as a draftsman and designer then as a field representative in quality and safety. He moved here from out of state to be near family. He likes his friendly neighborhood and shows up for many hobbies. He is gifted with a talent for music and shares it.

"Thoughts And Observations Of What I See"

Bob, 67, has been retired for several years after a career in transportation now really enjoys the amenities of this community. He has many hobbies and time to reflect on life. He showed up to explore and share interests in writing and photography.

"He Tried The Best He Could"

Ben, 68, moved to California to be near his family. He is a retired historian working mainly on the East Coast. He showed up here saying that retirement is the "best part of my life". He has liked getting involved in activities and social interactions. His hobbies include sharing a talent for music.

"Past, Present And Future"

Floyd, 64, was previously a restaurant owner, not ready to retire and working in a new profession. He has an interest in music as a hobby and shows up to share it in senior centers. Not interested in retirement at this time as he feels he still has too much to do. He gets his strengths and determination from his faith in God.

"What About Bob?"

Barney, 60, is still actively working. He is recently widowed and has family nearby. He shows up and is involved in local activities. He believes he can make a difference in his work. Christian faith guides his life. He says he is part of the problem and wants to be part of the solution.

"Smoke and Mirrors"

Dennis, 44, is a younger man who has been living with a serious disability that is getting progressively worse. Unable to work now after several years at a job he loved, he is a photographer and artist. He showed up and keeps busy using his creativity to design a car and restoring old cars like his father has done. He has put a lot of thought into life and is facing the future bravely. He hopes to write a book about his life.

"Adventurous"

Douglas, 77, worked many years in helping people in a search and rescue job. An avid sky diver for many years loved that as well as his humanitarian job. He showed up and founded an important sports league in his retirement community and is active in many activities. He says his wife changed his life for the better. His Christian faith guides him in his life.

MEN'S POINT OF VIEW

87

"To the 'Me' generation: look at yourself. Are you doing what is worthwhile?"

-- from an 85-year-old retired civil engineer, who even in retirement thinks there is not enough time to do it all.

MEN'S POINT OF VIEW

"About the younger generation, play it by ear and by kid; no one size fits all."

-- from an 87-year-old retired teacher.

"Nobody takes responsibility for actions – they make excuses. They need to be responsible for their own actions and see where they went wrong and change."

-- from a 73-year-old man who is still working
in his own company.

CHAPTER 11

YOUR LIFE REVIEW: LET'S GET STARTED

What is your life story? Have the stories of the men I interviewed here inspired you to start your own life review? We all have a story to tell about our lives. I thought it might be helpful to give you some space and a few key questions to start you along the path to your own life review.

Remember, there are no correct answers, only the ones that feel right to you. There are also no one-word (i.e., "yes" or "no") answers allowed. This whole process is about opening up your mind and your heart to the questions and letting your true feelings flow.

Feel free to use the next few pages to help get you in the proper mood and frame of mind to begin. Make notes, write an essay, draw pictures—whatever works to help you get started.

1.   What good, funny, and not so good memories do you have of growing up in your family?

2. What was the most significant time in your life? Why?

3. Who influenced you most in your life? Who have been the most significant persons in your life? Why?

4. Looking back what things in your life do you regret?

93

5. What do you want your family and the world to know about you—what do you want to be remembered for?

6. What is your absolutely favorite memory or memories?

95

ABOUT THE AUTHOR

Arloa Jane Walter was born in Wisconsin, raised in Minneapolis, Minnesota and then lived in the San Francisco Bay Area for most of her adult life. She earned a Bachelor of Science degree in Behavioral Sciences from the College of Notre Dame in Belmont, California (now called Notre Dame de Namur University) and a Masters of Social Work degree from the University of California at Berkeley. She is a wife, mother of three sons and a grandmother of seven. As a Licensed Clinical Social Worker, she has worked with the older population in all settings including as a case manager to those seniors living in their own homes, as a social worker in a hospital and in a skilled nursing facility, and as director of an adult day care center. Now retired, she spends her time volunteering and writing.

www.ingramcontent.com/pod-product-compliance
Lightning Source LLC
Chambersburg PA
CBHW061543050726
47593CB00002B/890